A Door in the Hive

Books by Denise Levertov

Poetry
The Double Image
Here and Now
Overland to the Islands
With Eyes at the Back of Our Heads
The Jacob's Ladder
O Taste and See
The Sorrow Dance
Relearning the Alphabet
To Stay Alive
Footprints
The Freeing of the Dust
Life in the Forest
Collected Earlier Poems 1940–1960
Candles in Babylon
Poems 1960–1967
Oblique Prayers
Poems 1968–1972
Breathing the Water
A Door in the Hive

Prose
The Poet in the World
Light Up the Cave

Translations
Guillevic/Selected Poems
Joubert/Black Iris (Copper Canyon Press)

Denise Levertov

A Door in the Hive

A NEW DIRECTIONS BOOK

Grateful acknowledgment is made to the editors and publishers of magazines in which some of the poems in this collection previously appeared: *Agni Review* (England), *American Poetry Review*, *Antaeus Journal, The Writer's Magazine, Clam* (England), *The Earlhamite, Gown* (Northern Ireland), *Green Mountain Review, Kentucky Poetry Review, Prism, Religion & Intellectual Life, Sandscript, Sequoia, Shenandoah, South Coast Poetry Review, The Southern California Anthology,* and *Tampa Review.* One poem also appeared in *Hill Field: Poems and Memoirs for John Montague* (Coffee House Press).

Author's Note: I would like to thank Nell Blaine for the generous loan of her house in Austria where some of these poems were written; Barbara Hyams for reading Rilke with me (in connection with the Rilke variations in *Breathing the Water* as well as the two in this volume); David Shaddock for advice and response; Yarrow Cleaves for response and typing. Additionally, I owe a retrospective debt of gratitude, in regard to earlier books, to Carlene Carrasco Laughlin, Phyllis Kutt, and Steven Blevins.

Manufactured in the United States of America.
New Directions Books are printed on acid-free paper.
First published clothbound and as New Directions Paperback 685 in 1989.
Published simultaneously in Canada by Penguin Books Canada Limited.

Library of Congress Cataloging in Publication Data
Levertov, Denise, 1923–
    A door in the hive / Denise Levertov.
       p.   cm.—(A New Directions paperbook)
    ISBN 0–8112–1119–3 (pbk. : alk. paper).—ISBN 0–8112–1118–5 (hard : alk. paper)
    I. Title.
PS3562.E8876D66   1989
811'.54–dc20
                                                    89–8304
                                                      CIP

New Directions Books are published for James Laughlin
by New Directions Publishing Corporation,
80 Eighth Avenue, New York 10011

Contents

A Door in the Hive

I

Once, in dream,
                    the boat
pushed off from the shore.
You at the prow were the man—
all voice, though silent—who bound
rowers and voyagers to the needful journey,
the veiled distance, imperative mystery.

All the crouched effort,
              creak of oarlocks, odor of sweat,
              sound of waters
              running against us
was transcended: your gaze
held as we crossed. Its dragonfly blue
restored to us
                    a shimmering destination.

I had not read yet of your Nile journey,
the enabling voice
drawing that boat upstream in your parable.
Strange that I knew
your silence was just such a song.

You were my mentor. Without knowing it,
I outgrew the need for a mentor.
Without knowing it, you resented that,
and attacked me. I bitterly resented
the attack, and without knowing it
freed myself to move forward
without a mentor. Love and long friendship
corroded, shrank, and vanished from sight
into some underlayer of being.
The years rose and fell, rose and fell,
and the news of your death after years of illness
was a fact without resonance for me,
I had lost you long before, and mourned you,
and put you away like a folded cloth
put away in a drawer. But today I woke
while it was dark, from a dream
that brought you live into my life:
I was in a church, near the Lady Chapel
at the head of the west aisle. Hearing a step
I turned: you were about to enter
the row behind me, but our eyes met
and you smiled at me, your unfocussed eyes
focussing in that smile to renew
all the reality our foolish pride extinguished.
You moved past me then, and as you sat down
beside me, I put a welcoming hand
over yours, and your hand was warm.
I had no need
for a mentor, nor you to be one;
but I was once more
your chosen sister, and you
my chosen brother.
We heard strong harmonies rise and begin to fill
the arching stone,
sounds that had risen here through centuries.

I am impatient with these branches, this light.
The sky, however blue, intrudes.
Because I've begun to see
there is something else I must do,
I can't quite catch the rhythm
of days I moved well to in other winters.
The steeple tree
was cut down, the one that daybreak
used to gild—that fervor of birds and cherubim
subdued. Drought has dulled
many a green blade.
                    Because
I know a different need has begun
to cast its lines out from me into
a place unknown, I reach
for a silence almost present,
elusive among my heartbeats.

If it's chariots or sandals,
I'll take sandals.
I like the high prow of the chariot,
the daredevil speed, the wind
a quick tune you can't
quite catch
        but I want to go
a long way
and I want to follow
paths where wheels deadlock.
           And I don't want always
to be among gear and horses,
      blood, foam, dust. I'd like
to wean myself from their strange allure.
I'll chance
the pilgrim sandals.

The nights pass, sleep and dreams, the ship rolling and creaking;
and days, clouds rolling soundlessly, creak of seabirds' wings
veering, battling headwinds. Nights, days, out on the main,
passage of years, decades, no landfall fragrance, peppery breeze.
Then a morning comes, this one, of light different
                                  as light in childhood
          when we opened our eyes to an altered ceiling,
          customary shadows absent,
          tenor of morning changed—afraid for a moment,
          then we knew, and jumped out of bed to look,
                and yes, the mystery
          was indeed the mystery of snowfall.

                    Today, awakening shows a color of ocean
unrecognized. And there are islands. Birds of new species
                    follow the wake.
The sky too is a sky not witnessed before, its hue
not imagined. Coastal villages, mountain contours almost
                    remembered—yet this
is not any place from which we left, some cognate rather. Travelers
not noticed before stand at the rail beside us. No sense of arrival;
a sense of approach. Some meet our eyes, we begin to speak, to hear
how their story—the long land journey, the port, delays, embarka-
                                    tion,
      storms, doldrums, then the seductive furrowing through time,
                            anything else
      receding, paling, fuzzy and then forgotten,
      only the sea present and real, and the ship nosing its way
under moon and sun—
                      was our own story.

Often, it's nowhere special: maybe
a train rattling not fast or slow
from Melbourne to Sydney, and the light's fading,
we've passed that wide river remembered
from a tale about boyhood and fatal love, written
in vodka prose, clear and burning—
the light's fading and then
beside the tracks this particular
straggle of eucalypts, an inconsequential
bit of a wood, a coppice, looks your way,
not at you, through you, through the train,
over it—gazes with branches and rags of bark
to something beyond your passing. It's not,
this shred of seeing, more beautiful
than a million others, less so than many;
you have no past here, no memories,
and you'll never set foot among these shadowy
tentative presences. Perhaps when you've left this continent
you'll never return; but it stays with you:
years later, whenever
its blurry image flicks on in your head,
it wrenches from you the old cry:
O Earth, belovéd Earth!
                              —like many another faint
constellation of landscape does, or fragment
of lichened stone, or some old shed
where you took refuge once from pelting rain
in Essex, leaning on wheel or shafts
of a dusty cart, and came out when you heard
a blackbird return to song though the rain
was not quite over; and, as you thought there'd be,
there was, in the dark quarter where frowning clouds
were still clustered, a hesitant trace
of rainbow; and across from that the expected
gleam of East Anglian afternoon light, and leaves

8

dripping and shining. Puddles, and the roadside weeds
washed of their dust. Earth,
that inward cry again—
Erde, du liebe . . .

At the jutting rim of the land he lives,
but not from ignorance,
not from despair.
He knows one extra step from his seaward
wide-open door would be
a step into salt air,
and he has no longing to shatter himself
far below, where the breakers
grind granite to sand.
No, he has chosen a life
pitched at the brink, a nest on the swaying
tip of a branch, for good reason:

dazzling within his darkness
is the elusive deep horizon. Here
nothing intrudes, palpable shade,
between his eager
inward gaze
and the vast enigma.
If he could fly he would drift forever
into that veil, soft and receding.

He knows that if he could see
he would be no wiser.
High on the windy cliff he breathes
face to face with desire.

II

Distanced

"If one's fate is to survive only sorrow, one has no right to the name survivor."

Shepherds in summer pastures
watched the invaders, a rectangular wave,
advance on the city far below. Smoke,
and towers falling. A straggling river
pouring from breached walls.
This high, no noises reached them.

They marvelled, they sorrowed.
Each had wished some day
to see for himself the city's
alien glories; all felt pity and dread.
They knew the river
was people fleeing.

But they could see no faces,
and no blood.

The vultures thrive,
clustered in lofty blue above
refuse-dumps where humans too
search for food, dreading
what else may be found.
Noble their wingspread,
hideous their descent
to those who know
what they may feast on:
sons, daughters.
And meanwhile,
the quetzal, bird of life, gleaming
green, glittering red, is driven
always further, higher,
into remote
ever-dwindling forests.

El Salvador: Requiem and Invocation

(A Libretto)

Not long after the murders of Archbishop Oscar Romero and of the three American nuns and a lay sister in El Salvador, I was asked by the composer Newell Hendricks to provide a text for him to work with in composing an oratorio. I suggested El Salvador as a theme, and these martyrdoms as a focus; and he was receptive to the idea. Drawing on my knowledge of Mexico and some research into Salvadoran history, I also obtained copies of letters written home by the four assassinated women as well as excerpts from Archbishop Romero's homilies. What I then attempted to write was not conceived as a poem so much as a working text for the composer—that is to say, I wanted to avoid certain nuances of rhythm and pitch in my words in order to produce something deliberately incomplete, something broadly sketched which would call precisely for that development the still-unwritten music would give it. Please see the note on pages 109–110 for further details of the piece's sources and development.—D.L.

El Salvador: Requiem and Invocation

Chorus (Words of Terror and Violence)

Blood Rape Kill Mutilate Death-squad Massacre
Torture Acid Order National Guard Thirst Pain
Crying Screaming Bloated Naked Helicopter
Slaughter Shoot Machine-gunned Beaten Vomit
Slash Burning Slit Bullhorns Sprayed Blinded
Bullets Machete Wounds Smash

(Phrases of Terror and Violence)
They cut off their heads They cut off their hands
They cut off their balls They cut off their breasts
Chopped up his face Hacking dead meat
The crops are burning 'Mama, they're burning
my dress!' 'The empire of hell' 'Hit them—hit them
again' 'We've hit them already—they'll
just die—leave them'
'I had a terrible thirst' 'The water was full of blood'
'Blood of my children' 'I kept drinking, drinking
the water. It was full of blood.'
'Kill the survivors' 'Tie their thumbs behind their
backs.' 'Acid is thrown in their faces.'
'We have seen too much, too many dead.'*
The air is black with smoke. No one is safe.

Voice of Questioner

O Mayan land! El Salvador!
What brought you to this time
of horror? Long ago
      it was not so—

* Actual quotations from eyewitness accounts

Chorus

Long ago
it was not so,
the land was generous,
the people lived at peace.
The land and people
were one, and lived
at peace:

Narrator

Long ago, in the far millenia,
already the Mayan folk were tending
pumpkins & chili,
corn and beans:
the earth was bountiful,
it gave freely:

Chorus

avocado, guava, papaya,
blackberry, elderberry,
tomato and calabash,
sapote, nopale—

Narrator

The people lived
with reverence, knowing
the daily mystery:
earth, sky, plants, men & women,
inseparable,
a single mystery:

The hoe, the digging stick,
were tools of a sacrament.
Prayers rose night & day
from the deep valleys,
from the lowlands,

17

from the mountainslopes
in the shimmering dust of months that are hot & dry,
in the great rains of summer
when thunder cracks its whip.
They knew the cycle, the rituals:
earth & sky,
fruits, animals,
humans:

Prayer (Chorus)

'O God,
Lord of the hills & valleys,
I am beneath thy feet,
beneath thy hands—
O God, my grandfather,
O God, my grandmother,
            God of the hills,
            God of the valleys,
my holy God:
                I make to you my offering
                with all my soul.
Be patient with me in what I am doing.

It is needful that you give me
all I am going to sow here,
here where I have my work,
my cornfield;
watch it for me,
guard my field for me, my *milpa,*
let it be safe,
from the time of sowing
to the time of harvest.'*

Narrator

And once a year
for five days there was silence—

* Kakehi Indian prayer

18

Chorus

Once a year
hide
in darkness
under roofs,
indoors—
do nothing,
don't eat
don't make love
don't speak,
hide
in darkness

the gods
are not here
not there
we know
nothing
we must
be still
be patient
in limbo,
holding our breath,
for then,
after silence
life will
continue,
earth & sky,
fruit and folk . . .

Narrator

And life continued, slow, long ago, the rhythms
of that slow dance, grandmother earth,
grandfather sky, their children & children's children.

Voice of Questioner

And then, and then?
  How did the horror begin?
Was it a thunderclap? Did men
blaspheme?

Narrator

Not with a thunderclap,
but yes,
with blasphemy:
but not the Maya blasphemed:
men from a far place,
a few, & a few, then more,
more—yet still
only a few, but powerful
with alien power—
came seeking gold,
        seeking wealth,
        denying
        the mystery of the land,
        the sacred harmony,
        breaking the rhythm
        taking the earth unto themselves
        to use it—

Chorus

To use it for money,
to send its fruits far away for money,
for others to use,
for people who had not seen the land
to eat and drink of its fruits,
to spend the money bought of its fruits:
the sacred fields given over
        to indigo
        to sugar
        to making rum out of sugar

to cotton
to coffee . . .
The land was raped,
forced to bear crops that
could not feed us.

Narrator

With pomp and circumstance
they came,
and new names for God:

they came speaking of goodness,
of good and evil;

they brought evil.
Our people were brought
under their domination, powerless.

Voices from Chorus

The lands of God our Golden Corn,
who nourishes us
were taken away from us,
taken away from Him:

Voices from Chorus

The lands of God our Dark Mother
the Cocoa Plant, *Madre Cacao*,
who gives us a sacred potion to drink,
were taken away from us,
taken away from Her.

Voices from Chorus

They made us use
cocoa-beans for small change.
Corn and cocoa and all plants
by which our bodies were sustained
                              or warmed

                        or clothed
and our spirits
                lightened or instructed—
all these were taken from us
and from our gods,
                the gods that dwelt in root and blossom,
                                in leaf and fruit—
taken, and put to strange uses.

Narrator

And time passed.
The conqueror's cattle
foraged and trampled the *milpas.*
Like hungry ghosts,
forced off the land,
the disinherited wandered to work
now here, now there,
or were rounded up,
their huts set on fire.
They were taken away into slavery.

Chorus

And time passed.
For one of the centuries
it was cane we served,
that turned into rum,
which whenever we could we drank
to make us forget
hunger and loss
and loss of the gods they said
the new god had conquered.

And time passed.
For one of the centuries
our slavery was to indigo.
Stench
of rotten indigo buzzing with flies

22

lay heavy over our compounds.
Brown hands
turned blue.
Fevers killed many.
Many escaped at night
to eat poison roots
or to hang themselves in the forest.

Narrator

And time passed.
As cane for rum
had supplanted the corn,
and then indigo
made more of a profit than rum,
now the dye gave place
to coffee.

Chorus

We worked, we worked, the cycle
of sun and rain continued but we
were hungry,
hungry, hungry,
our children were few,
they died,
our numbers dwindled,
yet there was no longer food enough in the land
for the land's own people.

Narrator

Thus the crops changed
as demand changed,
but the people,
the people were still enslaved.

Chorus

We were hungry, hungry, hungry, hungry,
hungry and enslaved.

Narrator (Staccato; like a huckster)

And the century
was the fifth since the conquest,
the 20th century,
the market for coffee
was big.
          For this was the century
that got where the others were going,
and made
          the whole world into a marketplace!

Chorus

And at last we could bear
no more: and the people,
we the poor
we the hungry
we the enslaved,
tried to throw off our chains—

tried when a peasant, our own brother,
Farabundo Martí
rose up to lead us,
tried
      to rise with him:

tried and failed,
crushed by the power of their guns,
money and guns,
their machine guns bought with the money
our labor provided, coffee
exchanged for money, money
given back in exchange for guns,
machine guns to murder the people to show

24

the people they cannot rebel, to keep
the people enslaved, working to grow
the coffee to sell for money the people
don't ever see, the money to buy
the machine guns . . . coffee money blood murder
machine guns buy sell enslaved . . .*

Narrator

But now among those
who long ago had come with the conquerors
bearing aloft the image of a God they said was good,
in whose name they and
the conquerors, soldiers of fortune,
took power,
              took power and gave to the people
not God's good but evil;
who crushed the people as they
crushed the old gods,
who came as priests of conquest—
now among these were heard
    new voices
    voices of mercy
    voices of pity
    voices of love for the poor;

Chorus

and now
the nuns, priests, bishops,
not only spoke but listened,

and listening gave
the great gift of attention,
and fed the hungry
not with scraps and crumbs of
    uncharitable charity

* Cacophonous babble ensues, followed by orchestral interlude

but with respect,
calling for justice.

Narrator

And strongest among them, a voice leading the chorus,
Oscar Romero, the Arch-
bishop, 'prince of the church,' whose riches
were faith, hope, and love,
who, day by day,
     week by week,
gathered testimony of terror,
of 'the insulted and injured'—

Romero

'the clamor of the people, the aching
of so much crime, the ignominy
of so much violence'†

Narrator

—and broadcast it, Sunday by Sunday

Chorus

—that no general
     no member of the Junta
     no National Guardsman
     no business tycoon
could claim innocence, ignorance;
no side of the great multifaceted
crime of oppression
would go undenounced.

---

† This and all subsequent quotations by Romero are taken from his
public statements.

Narrator

And each week he read
the roll of names of the newly dead—
of the men, women, and children
abducted, tortured, killed, disappeared
that week.
      He was Archbishop:
the junta's anger
smouldered.

Romero
ANTONIO FLORES
SANDRA MARITZA GALICIA
EVE CATALINA HERNANDEZ
DENIS ORLANDO GALLARDO
BORIS NAPOLEAN MARTINEZ
JAIME ANDRES LOPEZ CASTELLON
SONIA ELIZABETH MEJIA
JUAN RAMON PEREZ SANDOVAL
BLANCA ESTELA CONTRERAS
RAMIRO ENRIQUEZ
RAUL OMAR ROSALES CAMPOS
RICARDO ERNESTO ORELLANA
EDWIN CHAVEZ
ADILSON MELENDEZ SOMOZA
DEMESIO ZETINO RODRIQUEZ
LORI ROBERTO ORELLANA SANCHES
JOSE ROBERTO PONCE VELASQUEZ
JOSE GUIERMO CARPIO
MARCO ANTONIO CARCAMO DONA
ANTONIO DUBON SANCHEZ
ARISTIDES WILFREDO CASTILLO
EFRIAN MENJIVAR
YURI ELMER ARIA NOVOA
CLAUDIA INES CUELLAR COTO
JUAN MANUEL RODRIQUEZ
ADOLFO BERNAL MEJIA

MARIA CRISTINA JUAREZ
MARIA ALICIA PEREZ
ROSA MARGARITA JOAQUIN
LUIS ALBERTO DIAZ SERRANO
LUZ VASQUEZ MEJIA RIVERA
IVAN CUELLAS GIRON
CARLOS ARMANDO SERRANO
NAPOLEAN DE MONGE RIVERA
MARIA TERESA MANJIVAR
CARLOS ARMANDO MEDINA
HAYDEE YANIRA RIVERA
GORGE ANDRES CHACON SEQURA
ROXANA QUITANILLA
RENE SANTOS
EDUARDO SANTOS
ELMA MOJICA
SERGIO MOJICA SANTOS
WALTER SANTOS
DELMA SANTOS
MORENA SANTOS
BEATRIZ SANTOS
SONIA MOJICA
TOMMASA SANTOS
HERMINA SANTOS
ERASMO VLADIMIRO SANTOS
VENECIA AND VICTORIA SANTOS
ROSA SANTOS
TERESA SANTOS
ELBA SANTOS
ROSA MOJICA
MARCOS MOJICA SANTOS
HUGO MOJICA SANTOS . . .*

* Voice continues *diminuendo* behind chorus

Chorus

The pain, the murders,
the hunger, the tortures,
all continued,
and continue still,
and increase—

yet the voices that tell us
our broken bodies are not after all
worthless rubbish, but hold
sparks of the God—
                    these voices
begin to give us our freedom:

Half Chorus

Though we have lost
knowledge of old harmonies,
old ways we spoke to the earth,
                    sang to the sky—
though we have lost
the knowledge we had
        of grandfather, grandmother
        god in the ear of corn,
        god in the cocoa-bean,
        god the rain and
        god the sun—

Chorus

Yet now
our dignity grows in us
once more,
we believe
there is life in our land
to be lived,
that our anguish
moves us onward, forward towards
a time of justice . . .

Narrator

And time was passing,
quickly, quickly,
here in the small land of El Salvador
as in the rest of the troubled globe,
where wars and hunger and fear
convulse and contort
like vast and poisonous clouds
battling in nightmare skies
as the century's last quarter
hurtles toward the unknown—
and into this chaos
　　where daily among the people
　　priests and nuns risked with the rest
　　torture, 'disappearance,' mutilation,

Chorus

FATHER MARCIEL SERRANO
FATHER ERNESTO ABREGO
FATHER RUTILIO GRANDE
SISTER SYLVIA MARIBEL ARRIOLA . . .*

Narrator

and into this chaos arrived four women
out of the north—

Chorus

—out of that land
whose money and power and weapons
support our oppressors, and teach
the junta's killers
new ways of killing:
four Yanqui nuns—

---

* Chorus continues with additional names

Narrator

—arrived to join
their sisters and serve the people:
Ita, Maura, Jean, Dorothy.

Dorothy

'We have come to a land that
is writhing in pain . . .
Yet a land that's waiting, hoping,
yearning for peace.'*

Maura

'We came in answer
to a call. The need
is overwhelming.'*

Ita

'We came to live with the poor.
To be
evangelized by the poor.'*

Jean

'I was a lay missioner.
I came to give
two years of myself.
I was not planning to stay.'*

All Four

'We have come to a land that
is writhing in pain.
Yet a land that's waiting, hoping,
yearning for peace.'*

* These and all subsequent quotations by the four sisters are taken
from their letters.

31

Narrator

And Romero spoke to the soldiers,
the National Guard, the police,
        saying,

Romero

'Brothers, you belong
to our own people! You kill
your brother peasants!
Stop the killing—for no one
has to comply with immoral orders,
immoral laws.'†

Narrator

And Romero spoke to the government,
saying,

Romero

'Reforms mean nothing
when they are bathed
in so much blood.'†

Chorus

We are refugees
in our own country,
herded and huddled
now here, now there—

Sisters (Singly)

'We came to bring food and shelter'
'To search for the missing'
'To help in the struggle to break
out of the bonds
        of oppression
        and hunger
        and violence'—

Sisters (Together)

'in a land that is writhing in pain,
yearning for peace,'*

Chorus (Overlap echo effect)

So much blood
          So much blood

So many deaths
          So many deaths

So much courage
          So much courage

So much endurance
          So much endurance

So much faith
          So much faith

Chorus

We learned
how the old gods, our grandparents, long betrayed,
unite with the god our martyred friends
brought in their hearts to us: the crucified—
          who refused to be bought,
          who suffered like us,
          who returned from the dead.

Sisters (Together)

'In a land that is writhing in pain,
yearning for peace,'*

to suffer the powerlessness of the poor
and to go beyond it,

33

to discover,
to discover and to reveal

the power of that powerlessness.

Chorus (With irony)

Powerless, feathers in a whirlpool,
they were killed,
of course. (**Echo:** Of course, of course, of course . . .)

Voice of Questioner

O Mayan land! El Salvador!
what brought you to this time
of horror?

Narrator

Archbishop Romero gunned down
in the hospice for incurables,
named for Divine Providence:
his killers
chose their moment.
He fell
at the altar, saying
a requiem mass, saying
'Let us unite'—

Romero

'Let us unite in faith and hope
as we pray
for the dead
and for ourselves.'†

Narrator

A magnum slug,
his heart torn open,
a single shot,

34

a hired killer,
a distance of 20 meters.

Half Chorus

His killers
were ironic;
*but in martyrdom
is a seed of power!*

Narrator

The sisters, travelling
on their road of mercy,
were ambushed,
raped,
killed,
flung in a pit.

Half Chorus (Bitterly ironic)

Raped, killed, flung in a pit—
the usual way.
The soldiers
had practice.
*But in martyrdom
is a seed of power.*

Voice of Questioner

What do they ask,
the martyrs,
of those who hear them,
who know
the story, the cry,
who know what brought
our land to this grief?
What do their deaths demand?

Romero and Four Sisters

We ask that our story be known
not as the story of Salvador only;
everywhere, greed
exploits the people,
everywhere, greed
gives birth to violence,
everywhere, violence
at last is answered with violence:
   the desperate turn,
convulsed with pain,
to desperate means.

Half Chorus

Those who were martyred
bequeathed, a gift to the living,
their vision:
they saw, they told in their lives that violence
is not justice, that merciless justice
is not justice, that mercy
does not bind up
festering wounds,
but scrapes out the poison.

That 'no one has to comply
with immoral laws,'†

that power abused is powerless to crush
the spirit.

Half Chorus

Now we still writhe in agony,
violent against
the unceasing violence of greed,
the greed for profit, the greed for power,
the greed of faraway strangers
to hold the world's power in their hands.

Desperation
drives us: we take no joy
in bloodshed: our longing,
our longing, our longing,
is for Peace and the works of Peace:

even now in the hidden villages,
in the mountain camps,
schools for the people spring up
like corn in the ancient *milpas*—
play and knowledge for children,
dignity for women, hope for men,
poems and songs of the people:
all of this
is for Peace. For this
our martyrs died.
Their deaths
enjoin upon us, the living,
not to give up the vision
of lives freed from the lead weight
of centuries, clear of the stain
          of indigo, stench
          of fermenting sugar,
          whistle of whiplash,
          cramps of hunger,
          ache of lost dignity, loss
          of the ancient rhythms—
vision of simple peace,
sharing our minds, our labor, our soup,
teaching hope to our children,
putting behind us
the terror of centuries.

Chorus

Those who were martyred—
Romero,
          Maura,
                    Ita,

37

                    Dorothy,
                              Jean—
and those whose names
are lost along with their bodies—
all the Marias and Juans, the Josés and Pedros,
Elenas and Glorias—they tell us,
                    we in El Salvador, you
our sisters and brothers who know
the story,
all of us, all—
they tell us that horror
won't cease on the earth
till the hungry are fed,

that the fruits of the earth
don't grow that a few may profit,

that injustice here
is one with injustice anywhere,
all of us *are*
our brother's keepers,
members one of another,
responsible, culpable, and—

able to change.
This is the knowledge
that grows in power
out of the seeds of their martyrdom.

Romero and Four Sisters

Let us unite
in faith and hope
as we pray
for the dead
and for ourselves.

All

Let us unite
in faith and hope
as we pray:
as we pray for the dead
in faith and hope:
in faith and hope
as we pray:

as we pray for ourselves
for faith
as we pray
for hope.

The Book Without Words

(From a painting by Anselm Kiefer)

The gray waves gnash
their teeth of foam.

Behind this verge,
the barren plain,
seamed, fissured.

Ahead, limitless ocean.
The sky's low ceiling
bears down upon it,
dark and darkening.

Here at the end of land
(not earth but cinders)

was to have been given
the ultimate direction.
The sea-voyage was to begin.

And indeed the book
is here, a huge volume,
open and upright—
it levitates, close to the hiss of spume,

immutable, desolate, cast
in lead. Wordless.
If with great force its pages
were made to turn,
they would knock, unresonant,

one on another,
void upon void.
You have come to the shore.
There are no instructions.

Variation on a Theme by Rilke

(*The Book of Hours,* Poem 8)

Soon, the end of a century. Is the great scroll
being shaken, the scroll
inscribed by God and daubed with our lives' graffiti,

to raise this wind that churns
the sleep of listeners?
What holds aloft
that banner, that undeciphered legend?

Familiar powers extend towards it
their fingers of bone—
it lifts
        beyond reach,
an elusive kite.

And the wind
rises and rises, the powers
exchange dark looks, the sleepers
watch and listen.

                        Is there more parchment
wound, still, on the heavy spindle?
If, when the scroll unfurls, it reveals
a pallid, empty field,
                    what shall be written there?
Where, if we discover the runes continue,
shall we seek out
                their hierophant?

In California: Morning, Evening, Late January

Pale, then enkindled,
light
advancing,
emblazoning
summits of palm and pine,

the dew
lingering,
scripture of
scintillas.

Soon the roar
of mowers
cropping the already short
grass of lawns,

men with long-nozzled
cylinders of pesticide
poking at weeds,
at moss in cracks of cement,

and louder roar
of helicopters off to spray
vineyards where *braceros* try
to hold their breath,

and in the distance, bulldozers, excavators,
babel of destructive construction.

Banded by deep
oakshadow, airy
shadow of eucalyptus,

miner's lettuce,
tender, untasted,

and other grass, unmown,
luxuriant,
no green more brilliant.

Fragile paradise.

    . . . .

At day's end the whole sky,
vast, unstinting, flooded with transparent
mauve,
tint of wisteria,
cloudless
over the malls, the industrial parks,
the homes with the lights going on,
the homeless arranging their bundles.

    . . . .

Who can utter
the poignance of all that is constantly
threatened, invaded, expended

and constantly
nevertheless
persists in beauty,

tranquil as this young moon
just risen and slowly
drinking light
from the vanished sun.

Who can utter
the praise of such generosity
or the shame?

In their homes, much glass and steel. Their cars
are fast—walking's for children, except in rooms.
When they take longer trips, they think with contempt
of the jet's archaic slowness. Monastic
in dedication to work, they apply honed skills,
impatient of less than perfection. They sleep by day
when the bustle of lives might disturb their research,
and labor beneath fluorescent light in controlled environments
fitting their needs, as the dialects
in which they converse, with each other or with
the machines (which are not called machines)
are controlled and fitting. The air they breathe
is conditioned. Coffee and coke keep them alert.
But no one can say they don't dream,
that they have no vision. Their vision
consumes them, they think all the time
of the city in space, they long for the permanent colony,
not just a lab up there, the whole works,
malls, raquet courts, hot tubs, state-of-the-art
ski machines, entertainment . . . Imagine it, they think,
way out there, outside of 'nature,' unhampered,
a place contrived by man, supreme
triumph of reason. They know it will happen.
They do not love the earth.

Two Threnodies and a Psalm

I

It is not approaching.
It has arrived.
We are not circumventing it.

It is happening.
It is happening now.
We are not preventing it.
We are within it.

.

The sound of its happening
is splitting other ears.
The sight of its happening
is searing other eyes.
The grip of its happening
is strangling other throats.

.

Without intermission it spins,
without cessation we circle its edge
as leaf or crumb will float circling
a long time at the outer rim
before centripetal force
tugs it down.

II

The body being savaged
is alive.
It is our own.

While the eagle-vulture
tears the earth's liver,
while the heart-worm burrows
into earth's heart,

we are distant from what devours us
only as far as our extremities are from our minds,
which is no great distance.

　　　　　．

Extremities, we are in
unacknowledged *extremis*.
We feel only
a chill as the pulse of life
recedes.

We don't beat off the devouring beak,
the talons. We don't dig out what burrows
into our core. *It is not
our heart, we think* (but do not say).
*It is the world's, poor world, but I
am other*.

III

Our clear water
one with the infested water
　　　　　women walk miles to
　　　　　each day they live.
One with the rivers tainted with detritus
　　　　　　　　　　　of our ambitions,
and with the dishonored ocean.
Our unbroken skin
one with the ripped skin of the tortured,
　　　　　the shot-down, bombed, napalmed,
　　　　　the burned alive.
One with the sore and filthy skin of the destitute.

•

We utter the words
we are one
but their truth
is not real to us.

Spirit, waken
our understanding.
Out of the stasis
in which we perish,
the sullen immobility
to which the lead weight of our disbelief
condemns us,
only your rushing wind
can lift us.

•

Our flesh and theirs
one with the flesh of fruit and tree.

Our blood
one with the blood of whale and sparrow.

Our bones
ash and cinder of star-fire.

Our being
tinder for primal light.

•

Lift us, Spirit, impel
our rising
into that knowledge.

Make truth real to us,
flame on our lips.

47

Lift us to seize the present,
wrench it
out of its downspin.

Kin and Kin

For William Everson

Perhaps Jeffers was right, our species
best unborn, and once born
better soon gone, a criminal kind,
the planet's nightmare. Our going
would leave no hauntings at all, unless
to the last of those we've tamed or caged;
after those, a world
fierce in the hunt but free from malice
and free from remembrance.

Yet there have been the wise, the earthen elders
humble before the grass.
When from the torturers, picking their teeth
after a full meal, relaxed
after a full day of their routine job, we turn
to regard such others, remote as they are, yet kin—
as wheat and weed are kin, each
having root, stem, seed—or when
we hear some note of kindness
innocent of its own courage amid
the clamor of lies, it seems after all

there might be open to us, even now,
a chance to evolve, a swerve we could take,
a destiny still held out (if we would look)
in the Spirit's palm.

It's when we face for a moment
the worst our kind can do, and shudder to know
the taint in our own selves, that awe
cracks the mind's shell and enters the heart:
not to a flower, not to a dolphin,
to no innocent form
but to this creature vainly sure
it and no other is god-like, God
(out of compassion for our ugly
failure to evolve) entrusts,
as guest, as brother,
the Word.

III

Where Is the Angel?

Where is the angel for me to wrestle?
No driving snow in the glass bubble,
but mild September.

Outside, the stark shadows
menace, and fling their huge arms about
unheard. I breathe

a tepid air, the blur
of asters, of brown fern and gold-dust
seems to murmur,

and that's what I hear, only that.
Such clear walls of curved glass:
I see the violent gesticulations

and feel—no, not nothing. But in this
gentle haze, nothing commensurate.
It is pleasant in here. History

mouths, volume turned off. A band of iron,
like they put round a split tree,
circles my heart. In here

it is pleasant, but when I open
my mouth to speak, I too
am soundless. Where is the angel

to wrestle with me and wound
not my thigh but my throat,
so curses and blessings flow storming out

and the glass shatters, and the iron sunders?

Soutine (Two Paintings)

As if the forks themselves
were avid for the fish,
dead scrawny fish
on dead-white plate.
As if the red steps
were clutching the hill,
famished,
crawling toward the summit.
O desperate things,
living lives unheeded,
disbelieved
by those who made them!
O grey void, usurping
the abandoned cup's
parched hollow!

And houses lean, wavering,
to watch if the steps will ever
arrive, and what could there be,
up there,
to fulfil desire?

The Love of Morning

It is hard sometimes to drag ourselves
back to the love of morning
after we've lain in the dark crying out
O God, save us from the horror. . . .

God has saved the world one more day
even with its leaden burden of human evil;
we wake to birdsong.
And if sunlight's gossamer lifts in its net
the weight of all that is solid,
our hearts, too, are lifted,
swung like laughing infants;

but on gray mornings,
all incident—our own hunger,
the dear tasks of continuance,
the footsteps before us in the earth's
belovéd dust, leading the way—all,
is hard to love again
for we resent a summons
that disregards our sloth, and this
calls us, calls us.

Last night the stars had a brilliance more insistent
than I'd seen for months. The sword of Orion poised
ready to strike—one of the few constellations I know.
      Once for a short while
I lived by a lake. Each day a gentle man
who knew much about poetry, much about William Blake,
but spoke with a painful stutter, brought to my door
food, messages, friendship;
sometimes his two young sons came with him,
one of them just recovered from dangerous illness.
It snowed while I was there
and I took a photo that caught
the large loose flakes descending
among awestruck tall and straight young trees.
But mostly that winter it was so warm
by noon you could sit outdoors
and the Canada geese had halted
on their way south, encamped, like me, on the shore.
Heading out each day in captained hundreds
to forage, they returned at dusk,
troop by troop, and barked the day's luck to each other,
a multifold, intimate tribal lay . . .
In the cottage, where all was old, delicate, friendly,
I wrote a poem to the antique clock that for years
had peacefully kept its own time.
Before sleep I would stop outdoors:
the lake silent, no wind in the trees,
the throng of geese at rest, but always
a few of them stirring;
and the winter stars.
      Later the man and one of his sons
(I never found out which one, whether the boy
death had already fingered and left,
or the one more robust)
were killed by a drunken driver.

The wife and the lonely brother
moved away. 'Eating the bread of bitterness' was the phrase
that came to my mind. There had been
much love and kindness among those four.
        There are clusters, constellations,
one can perceive as grouped
but which suggest no figure of myth,
no meaning. The stars which give
a clue to the pattern
are too many light-years away, perhaps,
for our eyes, or our telescopes,
or even our inner vision.
Those we perceive can seem
to threaten us or implore, so insistently
their remote beauty glitters upon us,
and with such silence.

Two Mountains

*"To perceive the aura of an object,
we look at means to invest it with
the ability to look at us in return."*
Walter Benjamin

For a month (a minute)
I lived in sight of two mountains.
One was a sheer bastion
of pale rock. 'A rockface,' one says,
without thought of features, expression—
it's an abstract term.
        But one says, too,
'a stony-faced man,' or 'she maintained
a stony silence.' This mountain,
had it had eyes, would have looked always
past one or through one; its mouth,
if it had one, would purse thin lips,
implacable, ceding nothing, nothing at all.

The other mountain gave forth
a quite different silence.
Even (beyond my range of hearing)
it may have been singing.
Ravines, forests, bare rock that peaked, off-center
in a sharp and elegant cone or horn, had an air
of pleasure, pleasure in being.
At this one I looked and looked
but could devise
no ruse to coax it to meet my gaze.
I had to accept its complete indifference,
my own complete insignificance,
my self
        unknowable to the mountain
as a single needle of spruce or fir
on its distant slopes, to me.

58

the sacred bats
hang in their chosen grove,
     sinister old dustbags,
     charcoal gray,
doze upside down,
     alien, innocent.
Restless, like seals on a rock,
they nudge one another,
they slip off into air to circle
     the trees and
return, squeaking their utterance,
a fluttering language, and others, disturbed,
squeak in reproof.
     All day in the heat
they wait
for dusk and the high
invisible orchards.

If they could think
it would not be of us.

A Sound

1

An unexplained sound, today,
in the early sunlight
and no wind stirring the leaves,
of something breathing
                        surrounds the house,
quiet, regular, as of someone
peacefully dreaming; something close,
yet not located: one can't say,
'it comes from beneath the southwest window,'
for, go to the north window,
it breathes there too.

2

                    They say that once,
and in living memory, orchards of apricot,
nectarine, peach, filled this valley.
In spring it drifted in ruffles
of lacy white, of lacy pink.
And before that time, for centuries
months would go by each year when no human gaze
witnessed the changes here. Forest or grassland,
green to tawny and slowly
back to green as the seasons
paced in their circle-dance. The oaks
were thick on the hills.

3

Whatever was breathing nearby,
early today, I can't hear
now that the sun is high.
It woke, perhaps, and softly

60

removed itself. Or maybe
it turned in its sleep,
lowered itself to new depths of dream,
soundless. I think I shall hear it
breathing some day again. Or if I'm gone,
no matter—I think the sound
will recur. It need not be heard.

The bare trees
have made up their seed bundles.
They are ready now.
The warm brown light
pauses briefly, shrugs and moves on.
They are ready now
to play dead for a while.
I, human, have not as yet devised
how to obtain
such privilege.
Their Spring will find them rested.
I and my kind
battle a wakeful way
to ours.

On the young tree's highest twig,
a dark leaf, dry, solitary, left over
from winter, among the small new buds.
But it turns its head!
                       It's a hummingbird,
tranquil, at rest, taking time off
from the hummingbird world of swift intensities—
yet no less attentive. Taking
a long and secret look at the day,
like a child whose hiding-place
has not been discovered, who hasn't even
been missed. No hue and cry.
                       I saw
a leaf: I shall not betray you.

Lord, not you,
it is I who am absent.
At first
belief was a joy I kept in secret,
stealing alone
into sacred places:
a quick glance, and away—and back,
circling.
I have long since uttered your name
but now
I elude your presence.
I stop
to think about you, and my mind
at once
like a minnow darts away,
darts
into the shadows, into gleams that fret
unceasing over
the river's purling and passing.
Not for one second
will my self hold still, but wanders
anywhere,
everywhere it can turn. Not you,
it is I am absent.
You are the stream, the fish, the light,
the pulsing shadow,
you the unchanging presence, in whom all
moves and changes.
How can I focus my flickering, perceive
at the fountain's heart
the sapphire I know is there?

IV

A Woodcut

(*Jean Duvet, 1480–1561*)

St. John, as Duvet's angel leads him
(roused from his arbor beyond
the river's moored boats and conversing swans)
through clouds, above the earthly orchards,
writes as he walks. But when he reaches
burnished Jerusalem, thronged with the blessèd,
most of them upward-gazing in adoration, some
leaning their arms on a balustrade
to dreamily scan implicit horizons
level with their celestial vantage-point,

he kneels wordless, gazing too—upward, outward,
back at the angel (now behind him), downward, inward—
his ink-bottle slung at his hip
as before, but his notebook
vanished, perhaps discarded.

Men who planned to be hermits, hoped to be saints, arrived
in a round boat of wicker and skin at a pebbled cove.
Behind them, dangerous leagues of mist and wave
and behind those, a land belov'd and renounced. Before them,
beyond the slope of stones and the massed green
spears of iris, waited the island, habitation of birds
and of spirits unknown, dwellers in mounds and hummocks.

Under Columba's saltwashed toes, then jostled beneath
sacks of provisions, and briefly hidden under the coracle
brothers lifted to safety above the tideline, lay
this stone, almost a seabird's egg in form, in color
a white that, placed upon white, is revealed as pearl grey.
Now worn down by fourteen more centuries, its lustre
perhaps has increased, as if moonlight, patiently
blanching and stroking, had aided weather and water
in its perfecting.
                                    Hold the stone in your palm:
it fills it, warm when your need is for warmth,
cool when you seek the touch of shadow. Its weight
gives pleasure. One stone is not like another.

The Sculptor (Homage to Chillida)

A man who lives with his shadow
on equal terms,

who learns from his shadow the arcane power
of right-angles:
> ascension and lever,
> taproot and flower.

A man who transmutes
mass into fire: from red, gold; from gold, white—
> iron accepting rapture, moving,
> returning satisfied to its purpled
> black density, secretly curved.

Who permits stone
to acknowledge the inward void it compresses.

And to the impatient sea, the sea who knows everything,
gives immutable combs for its rushing tresses,

new gestures lifted
to the wind, new spouts
for the water curled by the wind
to pour itself into and leap from, shouting.

From behind the hill,
flowing through somber
palm, eucalyptus, web
of oakboughs, rises
light so pale a gold
it bathes in silver
the cool and still
air a single bird
stirs with tentative song.

The Braiding

The way the willow-bark
braids its furrows
is answered by the willow-branches
swaying their green leaf-weavings
over the river shallows,
assenting, affirming.

The mountain's spine, the cow's ridge,
the saddle dip,
                    high flanks,
spur of ranged
spruce, tail
to brush at flies, valley air
between them, and
                    nothing else.

Intricate and untraceable
weaving and interweaving,
dark strand with light:

designed, beyond
all spiderly contrivance,
to link, not to entrap:

elation, grief, joy, contrition, entwined;
shaking, changing,
                    forever
                            forming,
                                    transforming:

all praise,
        all praise to the
                        great web.

Blue-eyed Oberon prances
for joy in winter dusk,
the stars
are sparks from his deep, cold fur.
Motifs of Samoyed song
float forth from black lips.
                         For my part
I want the indoors, hot tea,
cherry jam. Yet I linger:
everything
instant by instant
intensifies,
dusk darker, stars wilder.
                         And Oberon,
strange-eyed Oberon,
meets my gaze in stillness
and holds it
                    before
he dances homeward,
dog and shaman.

So much is happening above the overcast!
Cloud poets, metaphysicians, essayists,
fabulists of the troposphere,
all at work, the material
their own metamorphic substance:
here a frank exposition, suds you could wash your clothes in,
there an abstract brocade that loops and swivels
in rivers of air. We glide low
across a forest, league on league
of trees in abundant leaf,
but white, silver-white, smudged with blue, tinged
with pink, like peonies—an entire summer
conjured in milky vapor, smoke of alabaster, slivers
of pearl. League on league
to a horizon more remote
than earth's horizons. Fading now,
curling, unfolding, imperceptibly flowing,
the blush paling. Dense thickets migrate
slowly across the fertile cloud-savannah, browsing.
And far aloft, in the sky's own sky, reclined,
the shepherd moon, propped on one elbow, watches
the flocks of drowsy cloud-lambs nibble their way out of being:
for darkness, even here, is gathering; the lunar gaze
dilates and begins to gleam,
while our enormous air-bus, throbbing west and south,
seems to tarry, fleck of metallic dust,
in this firmament where dreamy energies
sculpt themselves and winnow
epic epiphanies.

Tufts of brassy henna in the palm's
shaggy topknot—O Palm,
I like it, I like it!
                              And the dingy underlayer,
bedraggled skirt, tattered collar
around your furrowed neck, or is it your body,
that stout column?
                              You stay awake
all night every night
and tonight will be full moon. It's March,
and the ground beneath you
crunches under bicycle tires
where you littered it with your fruit,
those shiny brown things—I must take
a nutcracker to one some day, are they edible?
You let them fall
like a kid in the movies dropping a trail of popcorn.
                              Are you asleep up there,
your tousled green uncombed,
sunning yourself? Your way of paying
no attention, feline, and yet
strutting your crazy finery fit to kill,
I like it, I like it.

August Houseplant

Is there someone,
                 an intruder,
in my back yard? That slight
scraping sound again—only a cat
maybe?
         —I look from the screendoor:
Ah! It's you, dear leaves,
only you, big, wildly branching leaves
of the philodendron,
summering on the deck,
           touching the floor of it, feeling
          the chair,
              exploring.
As if you knew
            fall is coming, you seem to desire
    everything that surrounds you,
           all of air,
             all of light,
               all of shade.
How am I going to carry you in,
when it gets cold?
            It's not
that I can't manage the weight
of your pot of earth, though it's heavy.
It's those long, ever-longer, reaching arms
that don't fit through the door.
            And when you're manoeuvered in,
how small the room will become;
       how can I set you
            where your green questions
won't lean over human shoulders, obscuring
books and notepads, interrupting
trains of thought
           to enquire,
           mutely patient,
           about the walls?

Old chimney bricks, dull red,
sometimes charred in a manner resembling
the way some painters shade
tone into deeper tone:
I'm using them to mark
a new-dug bed where yesterday,
weak and uncertain-looking,
small annuals were planted. Things
get moved around, purposes
redefined.
The bricks aren't beautiful—but time
may change them, after their years
of heat and smoke. Time in the rain.

The nearest leaves, outside the glass,
let through no light

but those beyond them
are so filled with ecstatic green
it brims over, cloud of brilliance,
                    hovering ocean, glowing
          behind the dark others

that sway, ornate, specific, lobed, opaque,
each with its destiny,

defined upon that dazzling screen
which seems the very source,
for this hour,
of illumination.

v

On the Parables of the Mustard Seed

*(Matthew 17.20, Mark 4.30–32,
Luke 13.18–19)*

Who ever saw the mustard-plant,
wayside weed or tended crop,
grow tall as a shrub, let alone a tree, a treeful
of shade and nests and songs?
Acres of yellow,
not a bird of the air in sight.

No, He who knew
the west wind brings
the rain, the south wind
thunder, who walked the field-paths
running His hand along wheatstems to glean
those intimate milky kernels, good
to break on the tongue,

was talking of miracle, the seed
within us, so small
we take it for worthless, a mustard-seed, dust,
nothing.
          Glib generations mistake
the metaphor, not looking at fields and trees,
not noticing paradox. Mountains
remain unmoved.

Faith is rare, He must have been saying,
prodigious, unique—
one infinitesimal grain divided
like loaves and fishes,

as if from a mustard-seed
a great shade-tree grew. That rare,
that strange: the kingdom

                    a tree. The soul
a bird. A great concourse of birds
at home there, wings among yellow flowers.
The waiting
kingdom of faith, the seed
waiting to be sown.

The borderland—that's where, if one knew how,
one would establish residence. That watershed,
that spine, that looking-glass . . . I mean the edge
between impasto surface, burnt sienna, thick,
       striate, gleaming—swathes and windrows
       of carnal paint—
       or, canvas barely stained,
       where warp and weft peer through,

and fictive truth: a room, a vase, an open door
giving upon the clouds.

A step back, and you have
the likeness, its own world. Step to the wall again,
and you're so near the paint you could lick it,
you breathe its ghostly turpentine.
                    But there's an interface,
immeasurable, elusive—an equilibrium
just attainable, sometimes, when the attention's rightly poised,
where you are opulently received
by the bravura gestures hand and brush
proffer (as if a courtier twirled
a feathered velvet hat to bow you in)
and yet, without losing sight of one stroke,
             one scrape of the knife,
you are drawn through *into* that room, into
its air and temperature.

Couldn't one learn to maintain
that exquisite balance more than a second?
                  (One sees even
the pencilled understrokes, and shivers
in pleasure—*and* one's fingertips
touch the carpet's nubs of wool, the cold fruit in a bowl:
one almost sees
what lies beyond the window, past the frame, beyond . . .

85

Annunciation

'Hail, space for the uncontained God'
From the Agathistos Hymn,
Greece, VIc

We know the scene: the room, variously furnished,
almost always a lectern, a book; always
the tall lily.
        Arrived on solemn grandeur of great wings,
the angelic ambassador, standing or hovering,
whom she acknowledges, a guest.

But we are told of meek obedience. No one mentions
courage.
        The engendering Spirit
did not enter her without consent.
           God waited.

She was free
to accept or to refuse, choice
integral to humanness.

Aren't there annunciations
of one sort or another
in most lives?
        Some unwillingly
undertake great destinies,
enact them in sullen pride,
uncomprehending.
        More often
those moments
    when roads of light and storm
    open from darkness in a man or woman,
are turned away from

in dread, in a wave of weakness, in despair
and with relief.
Ordinary lives continue.
                    God does not smite them.
But the gates close, the pathway vanishes.

———————————

She had been a child who played, ate, slept
like any other child—but unlike others,
wept only for pity, laughed
in joy not triumph.
Compassion and intelligence
fused in her, indivisible.

Called to a destiny more momentous
than any in all of Time,
she did not quail,
                    only asked
a simple, 'How can this be?'
and gravely, courteously,
took to heart the angel's reply,
perceiving instantly
the astounding ministry she was offered:

to bear in her womb
Infinite weight and lightness; to carry
in hidden, finite inwardness,
nine months of Eternity; to contain
in slender vase of being,
the sum of power—
in narrow flesh,
the sum of light.
                    Then bring to birth,
push out into air, a Man-child
needing, like any other,
milk and love—

but who was God.

This was the minute no one speaks of,
when she could still refuse.

A breath unbreathed,
                    Spirit,
                              suspended,
                                        waiting.

———————————

She did not cry, 'I cannot, I am not worthy,'
nor, 'I have not the strength.'
She did not submit with gritted teeth,
                                   raging, coerced.
Bravest of all humans,
                    consent illumined her.
The room filled with its light,
the lily glowed in it,
                    and the iridescent wings.
Consent,
          courage unparalleled,
opened her utterly.

The certainty of wings: a child's bold heart,
not, good little *Schul*-boy, Torah or Talmud
gave it to you, a practical vision:
wings were needed, why should people
plod forever on foot, not glide like herons
through the blue and white
promise unfolding
over their heads, over
the river's thawing?
Therefore the pedlar. (But why did they not
avail themselves of his wares?)

My father, as a child, sees the magic pedlar Marc Chagall was also to see a few years later. The one intuited that he carried wings, the other painted him, wingless but floating high over Vitepsk.

Later, *ochetz moy,* when you discovered
wings for your soul, the same bold heart
empowered you. From Prussia east and
    southward
verst after *verst* you willed the train to go
               faster,
skimming the rails home to the Dnieper valley.
You bore such news, so longed-for,
fulfilling a hope so ancient
it had almost become dry parchment,
             not hope any more.

My father, as a student, discovers the Messiah,

At the station you hailed a *droshky,*
greeted the driver like a brother. At last
there was the street, there was the house:
but when you arrived
they would not listen.
They laughed at you. And then they wept.
But would not listen.

and hurries home with the good news,

but is not believed.

89

Even in her nineties she recalled
the smooth hands of the village woman
who sometimes came from down the street
and gently, with the softest
of soft old flannel,
soaped and rinsed and dried
her grubby face, while upstairs
the stepmother lay abed bitterly sleeping,
the uncorked opiate bottle
wafting out sticky sweetness
into a noontime dusk.
Those hands, that slow refreshment,
were so kind, I too,
another lifetime beyond them,
shall carry towards my death
their memory,
grateful, and longing
once again to feel them soothe me.

Nativity: An Altarpiece

The wise men are still on the road, searching,
crowns and gifts packed in their saddlebags.

The shepherds are still asleep on the hill, their woolen
caps pulled over their ears, their campfire low.

It's the wondering animals, ox and ass, unused
to human company after dark, who witness,

alone with Mary and Joseph, the birth; who hear
the cry, the first cry

of earthly breath drawn through the newborn lungs
of God.
        And the cord is cut, and the shepherds
that selfsame moment have sprung to their feet

in a golden shower of angels, terrified, then
rejoicing. They lope downhill to the barn

to see their Redeemer. A cloud of
celestial music surrounds them.

                    The wise men
are still far off, alone on the road with a star.

But the ox and the ass
are kneeling already, the Family's oldest friends,

in the glow of light that illumines the byre, the straw,
their eyes and the human eyes—a glow

shed from no source but the living Child Himself.

To look out over roofs
of a different city—

steaming tiles, chimney pots, mansards,
the gleam on distant spires
after a downpour—

To look out
(and the air freshens)
and say to oneself,
Today . . .

Somewhere, married and in love,
we walked through streets planted with linden trees.
There were ramparts, buttresses, ancient fragments
bonded with newer masonry that was old too.
The warmth of the day just ending
stretched itself on the stones, a golden dog.
People were strolling, there were no cars to speak of,
and we, we were only passing through.
What chance imperative held us on course
toward what train? Nothing I can remember,
no better city.
                    Quiet avenues. Lamps coming on.
The sky still full of light.
I can't remember arriving nor leaving,
and even while we were there it seems
we were somewhere else, inattentive. But the lindens
were blossoming, their perfume, mysterious, pianissimo,
filled the whole town: every few years that remembrance
briefly returns, as if
a fragment of dream; but I know
it was history, a bit of my life,
a bit of the life of Europe. The past.
We failed to linger—as if the lindens
only spoke over this gulf of time.

Where the stone steps
falter and come to an end
but the hillside rises
yet more steeply,
obtruded roots of the pines
have braided themselves
across the path to continue
the zigzag staircase.
In times past the non-human—
plants, animals—
often, with such gestures,
intervened in our lives,
or so our forebears
believed when all lives were seen
as travellings-forth of souls.
One can perceive
few come here now—
it's nothing special,
not even very old,
a naive piety,
artless, narrow. And yet
this ladder of roots
draws one onward, coaxing
feet to become
pilgrim feet, that climb
(silenced by layers
of fallen needles,
but step by step
held from sliding)
up to the last
cross of the calvary.

The Past (II)

'The witnesses are old things, undimmed, dense
With the life of human hands'
                                    Czeslaw Milosz

My hand on chiseled stone, fitting
into the invisible
                          print of the mason's own
                          where it lay
a moment of that year the nave
was still half-risen, roofless . . .

There's a past that won't suffice:
years in billions,
walls of strata. My need roams
history, centuries not aeons.
And replica is useless.

The new dust
floated past, his mate
from the scaffolding reached down
for the water-jug.

                          This stone
or another: no inch of all
untouched. Cold, yes,

but that human trace
will burn my palm.
This is a hunger.

The mountain trembles in the dark lake,
its golden cliffs dipping
from almost-sunset light
deep into almost-evening waters.
Round them the forest
floats, brushstrokes
                    blurred just a little.

Death and the past
move closer, move
away again and once more
come closer, swaying, unhurried,
like the sound
of cowbells wandering
down the steep pastures.

Midnight Gladness

'Peace be upon each thing my eye takes in,
Upon each thing my mouth takes in.'
                    Carmina Gadelica

The pleated lampshade, slightly askew,
dust a silverish muting of the lamp's fake brass.
My sock-monkey on the pillow, tail and limbs asprawl,
weary after a day of watching sunlight
             prowl the house like a wolf.
Gleams of water in my bedside glass.
Miraculous water, so peacefully
waiting to be consumed.

The day's crowding arrived
at this abundant stillness. Each thing
given to the eye before sleep, and water
at my lips before darkness. Gift after gift.

VI

St. Thomas Didymus

In the hot street at noon I saw him
                              a small man
          gray but vivid, standing forth
                              beyond the crowd's buzzing
holding in desperate grip his shaking
                              teethgnashing son,

and thought him my brother.

I heard him cry out, weeping, and speak
                              those words,
Lord, I believe, help thou
                    mine unbelief,

and knew him
          my twin:

a man whose entire being
                    had knotted itself
into the one tightdrawn question,
                              Why,
why has this child lost his childhood in suffering,
                    why is this child who will soon be a man
tormented, torn, twisted?
                    Why is he cruelly punished
who has done nothing except be born?

The twin of my birth
                    was not so close
as that man I heard
                    say what my heart
sighed with each beat, my breath silently
                              cried in and out,
in and out.

After the healing,
                    he, with his wondering
newly peaceful boy, receded;
                                        no one
dwells on the gratitude, the astonished joy,
                                        the swift
acceptance and forgetting.
                              I did not follow
to see their changed lives.
                              What I retained
was the flash of kinship.
                              Despite
all that I witnessed,
                    his question remained
my question, throbbed like a stealthy cancer,
                                        known
only to doctor and patient. To others
                                        I seemed well enough.

So it was
            that after Golgotha
                              my spirit in secret
lurched in the same convulsed writhings
                                        that tore that child
before he was healed.
                    And after the empty tomb
when they told me He lived, had spoken to Magdalen,
                                                told me
that though He had passed through the door like a ghost
                                        He had breathed on them
the breath of a living man—
                              even then
when hope tried with a flutter of wings
                                        to lift me—
still, alone with myself,
                    my heavy cry was the same: *Lord,*
I believe,
            help thou mine unbelief.

102

I needed
        blood to tell me the truth,
the touch
        of blood. Even
my sight of the dark crust of it
                round the nailholes
didn't thrust its meaning all the way through
                    to that manifold knot in me
that willed to possess all knowledge,
                refusing to loosen
unless that insistence won
            the battle I fought with life.

But when my hand
        led by His hand's firm clasp
entered the unhealed wound,
            my fingers encountering
rib-bone and pulsing heat,
           what I felt was not
scalding pain, shame for my
           obstinate need,
but light, light streaming
           into me, over me, filling the room
as if I had lived till then
           in a cold cave, and now
coming forth for the first time,
           the knot that bound me unravelling,
I witnessed
        all things quicken to color, to form,
my question
        not answered but given
                its part
in a vast unfolding design lit
        by a risen sun.

When he improvised, from what
unpremeditated congeries of wisdoms
did the sounds appear, woven
like laser tracings on the screen of air?
Music out of 'nowhere,' that granary,
that palace of Arabian serpents,
of sleek rats plush as
young seals. What do words, too,
do there, the real ones,
while we dally with their pale
understudies, or swim
through choppy floods, too busy
with breathing to summon them?
Could we live there? Is it dark?
Could the grain shoals
not light us with their gold sheen?
Invisible hive, has it no small door
we could find if we stood
quite still and listened?

Down through the tomb's inward arch
He has shouldered out into Limbo
to gather them, dazed, from dreamless slumber:
the merciful dead, the prophets,
the innocents just His own age and those
unnumbered others waiting here
unaware, in an endless void He is ending
now, stooping to tug at their hands,
to pull them from their sarcophagi,
dazzled, almost unwilling. Didmas,
neighbor in death, Golgotha dust
still streaked on the dried sweat of his body
no one had washed and anointed, is here,
for sequence is not known in Limbo;
the promise, given from cross to cross
at noon, arches beyond sunset and dawn.
All these He will swiftly lead
to the Paradise road: they are safe.
That done, there must take place that struggle
no human presumes to picture:
living, dying, descending to rescue the just
from shadow, were lesser travails
than this: to break
through earth and stone of the faithless world
back to the cold sepulchre, tearstained
stifling shroud; to break from *them*
back into breath and heartbeat, and walk
the world again, closed into days and weeks again,
wounds of His anguish open, and Spirit
streaming through every cell of flesh
so that if mortal sight could bear
to perceive it, it would be seen
His mortal flesh was lit from within, now,
and aching for home. He must return,
first, in Divine patience, and know

105

hunger again, and give
to humble friends the joy
of giving Him food—fish and a honeycomb.

Lent 1988

Variation on a Theme by Rilke

(The Book of Hours, Book I, #15)

With chips and shards, rubble of being,
we construct
            not You but our hope of You.
We say—we dustmotes in the cosmos—
'You dome, arching above us!':
as if You were the sanctuary
by which we seek to define You.

Our cities pulverize, proud technologies
spawn catastrophe. The jaws of our inventions
snap down and lock.
                  Their purpose will be forgotten;
Time is aeons
and we live in minutes,
flies on a windowpane.

Who can conceive the span of You,
great vault, ribbed cauldron slung beneath the abyss,
cage of eternity?

Metaphors shatter, mirrors of poverty.

But something in us, while the millennia
monotonously pass
            and pass,
hungers to offer up
our specks of life as fragile tesserae
towards the vast mosaic—temple, eidolon;

to be, ourselves, imbedded in its fabric,
as if, once, it was from that we were broken off.

Notes

3 'To Rilke.' The allusion is to Rilke's prose piece 'Concerning the Poet' (*Where Silence Reigns,* New Directions).

4 'To R.D., March 4th 1988.' Robert Duncan died on February 3, 1988.

8 'For Instance.' The German quotation is from the ninth of Rilke's *Duino Elegies.*

14 'Land of Death-Squads.' My source was a quotation in a review of Jonathan Maslow's *Bird of Life, Bird of Death.* His focus in that book was on Guatemala, where he sought the quetzal in the dwindling forests; but of course the bodies of the 'disappeared' have been found in garbage dumps in other countries as well.

15 'El Salvador: Requiem and Invocation' was performed in May 1983 at Sanders Theatre, Harvard University, by the Back Bay Chorale, with soloists, and the Pro Arte Chamber Orchestra, conducted by the late Larry Hill—these two groups having commissioned the work. I had supplied the composer Newell Hendricks with the text in three installments, and he had worked on the music in that same sequence; the joint project took around a year for us to complete. Until a final rehearsal I did not hear the music, except for a brief orchestral rehearsal tape, as I was in California during the rehearsal period. I had, however, included in my text a few 'stage directions,' as it were; for in order to meet the challenge of my task at all I had to *imagine* the music in some degree. Thus, with the opening words and phrases I included the suggestion not only that they were for chorus but also that their sounds be loud, harsh, cacophonous; or elsewhere that voices overlap and die away into silence, or perhaps be followed by an orchestral interlude. Newell followed through on all my concepts most intuitively, and produced what I and the audience felt was a very strong and remarkable piece of music.

The basic models in my listening experience were the Bach Passions and various Handel and Haydn oratorios. The Narrator, then, plays a role equivalent to that of the Evangelist in the St. Matthew or St. John Passion music. The Chorus represents the people of El Salvador. Occasionally a solo voice emerges from the chorus as an unspecified Questioner. And then there are the solo voices of the Archbishop and the four women.

The narrative line—after the initial outburst of violent words and sounds representing the extremity of El Salvador's present condition—moves from pre-Columbian times through a condensed history of the intervening centuries (which could equally be that of other Central American countries) to very recent events. During the pre-Columbian passages I adapted some actual Mayan prayers; and when I came to contemporary times, I quoted directly from Archbishop Romero's sermons and from the letters by Sisters Dorothy, Maura, and Ita and lay worker Jean, supplied to me by the Maryknoll Sisters. At one point in the text, Romero intones the names of civilians known to have been killed during the previous week: these are actual names, many of them, in this instance, belonging to members (mainly children) of a single family. It is an authentic, typical sampling of those weekly listings of murders done by right-wing death-squads which the Archbishop had the great courage to announce. Similarly, the list, at another point in the text, of priests and nuns murdered in the same manner consists of actual names. It should have been much longer, to be really representative.

The audience at the first performance of the oratorio in 1983 was provided with a program published by the Back Bay Chorale which included the text together with forewords by the composer, the conductor, myself, and the artist Michael Mazur who created a visual setting for the event, designed the program cover, and also sang as a member of the Chorale. A new edition was subsequently printed as a contribution to the organizations which are working to help Salvadoran and Guatemalan refugees, develop the ecumenical Covenant of Sanctuary movement, raise public awareness of the true situation, and give medical aid and moral support to the Salvadoran and other Central American people, as well as to protest United States military intervention. Copies were provided free to these organizations (and to a few individuals) for them to sell at whatever price they deemed appropriate.

44 'Those Who Want Out.' '. . . that the earth is an inert lump of matter, that our relationship to it is merely utilitarian, even that we might find a paradise outside it in space colonies. Such monstrous aberrations of thought are symptoms of the enchantment which blinds us to reality.'—John Michell, *The Earth Spirit: Its Ways, Shrines, & Mysteries* (Avon Books, New York 1975).

INDEX OF TITLES & FIRST LINES

New Directions Paperbooks – A Partial Listing

For complete listing request free catalog from
New Directions, 80 Eighth Avenue, New York 10011

† Bilingual

For complete listing request free catalog from
New Directions, 80 Eighth Avenue, New York 10011

† Bilingual